How to Attract Wealth, Health, Love, and Luck into Your Life Immediately

How to Attract Wealth, Health, Love, and Luck into Your Life Immediately

◆

A Concise Manual for Personal Success

AIMAN A. AL-MAIMANI

iUniverse, Inc.
New York Lincoln Shanghai

How to Attract Wealth, Health, Love, and Luck into Your Life Immediately
A Concise Manual for Personal Success

Copyright © 2006 by Aiman A. AL-Maimani

All rights reserved. No part of this book may be used or reproduced by any means, graphic, electronic, or mechanical, including photocopying, recording, taping or by any information storage retrieval system without the written permission of the publisher except in the case of brief quotations embodied in critical articles and reviews.

iUniverse books may be ordered through booksellers or by contacting:

iUniverse
2021 Pine Lake Road, Suite 100
Lincoln, NE 68512
www.iuniverse.com
1-800-Authors (1-800-288-4677)

This book is not intended to be a substitute for medical or professional treatment. It is a concise guide for personal success based on the author's own experiences, observations, reading, and education.

ISBN-13: 978-0-595-38363-4 (pbk)
ISBN-13: 978-0-595-67614-9 (cloth)
ISBN-13: 978-0-595-82736-7 (ebk)
ISBN-10: 0-595-38363-7 (pbk)
ISBN-10: 0-595-67614-6 (cloth)
ISBN-10: 0-595-82736-5 (ebk)

Printed in the United States of America

To my parents, who strove to teach me how to achieve success in this life. Their love supported me through happy times as well as sad ones.

Contents

Preface xi
CHAPTER 1   Introduction to Success 1
CHAPTER 2   The Law of Quantum Physics 7
CHAPTER 3   Positive Thinking Power 13
CHAPTER 4   Keep in Mind These Universal Laws 17
CHAPTER 5   The Law of Attraction 23
CHAPTER 6   Activating the Law of Attraction 35
CHAPTER 7   Control Your Own Life with NLP 45
CHAPTER 8   Be a Moving Success on the Globe 55
CHAPTER 9   Additional Tools to Enhance Your Success 61
One Final Word 67
References and Recommended Materials 69
APPENDIX A   Exercise 1 75
APPENDIX B   Exercise 2 83
APPENDIX C   Exercise 3 87
APPENDIX D   Ten-Year Goals 89
APPENDIX E   Sample Statements for the Law of Attraction 93
Index 95

Acknowledgments

I would like to offer my greatest thanks to everyone who helped me make this book an easy blueprint for success. To my parents, wife, children, and friends, who have supported me fully in the production of this book.

Special thanks are due to the great teachers—Brian Tracy, Dr. Stephen Covey, Dr. Michael Losier, Anthony Robbins, Lynn Grabhorn, Dr. Salah Alrashed, and Dr. Ibrahim Elfiky. I would also like to extend my thanks to Mark E. Johnson for the photos and diagrams that appear throughout this book.

Preface

This book is a concise manual for personal success in today's challenging world. Chapter 1 reviews how we perceive our own future. People tend to consider past experiences, whether successes or failures, to be predictions of the future. Wise men and women will look at success and benefit from strategies and skills they developed through past experience. However, the difficulty arises when people look at past failures that prevent them from trying again, going beyond those failed experiences, and thinking that there may be other approaches to achieve success.

The truth about failure is that it is an experience, and whatever result we got from it should be used to help us avoid similar shortfalls in the future. Treating failures this way strengthens us and lets us focus our compass toward our future goals much more precisely.

Chapter 2 examines the main points of the law of quantum physics and how it provides a comprehensive explanation of the dynamics between similar energies [thoughts or ideas and the physical representation of those ideas or thoughts] which will resonate with similar frequencies. Quantum physics can bless us with the choices between what we want and what we hate. If we want something, then our wanting will help us achieve that goal. If we hate something, then our hate works against us to bring what we hate to us as well. This universal law does not differentiate between the two situations as it has its own rule of vibrating similar things together. This is why it is important to represent what we hate in terms of something we want. For example, instead of hating to be fat we should love to be fit, slim, and healthy.

To help us alter the negative impact of law of quantum physics when we hate something, chapter 3 promotes positive thinking and discusses its benefits in managing and controlling our energy flows. Positive thinking saves and doubles our momentum. It extends beyond that when it converts negative energies to useful ones. Positive thinking gathers more energy, combining and bringing more positive power to the person. On the other hand, negative thinking accumulates negative energies that will eventually create a rolling snowball of negativity that destroys focus and leads to dramatic confusion and a lack of concentration. The universe is fair—it simply replies in the same way we play the game.

In chapter 4, I have included some additional universal laws that influence our actions and trigger our luck on our journey to the future. It shows you how our internal notion of the world in our mind shapes our external realization of the world around us. In another word, our perception of the external world is a reflection and a projection of our internal view of the world.

The law of attraction is often explained as an amazing tool which helps one reach one's goal at a speed that will only be believed once the reader tries to use it on his or her goals. The program set forth in this book requires twenty-one days to charge the brain with the required focus, energy, and goal achievement at rate higher than usual. You need to be committed to get what you want and to see the result you are waiting for.

To help you continue your progress on the road of success and to become more effective in this life, I have supplied a concise review of Neuro-Linguistic Programming (NLP) technique as the next step for you to follow. This science will enable you to have full control of your memories, feelings, imaginations, perception, body language, their behaviors, and actions.

Also, I have included some additional tools to help you broaden your vision, and consequently, I provided a list of references and recommended readings.

My promise in this material is to unlock your potential and to create a new mindset willing and confident of achieving any goal in life. If anyone can manage to achieve his or her dreams, then YOU can, too.

I assure you that YOU are a lucky and a unique person. By choosing and coming across this material, you will learn the best techniques to achieve your goals at amazing super speed with minimal effort.

I wish you best of luck in this book, and I hope you enjoy every topic as you progress on the material and exercises. I believe that you will have the ability to dream more and to achieve much more than you ever have thought before.

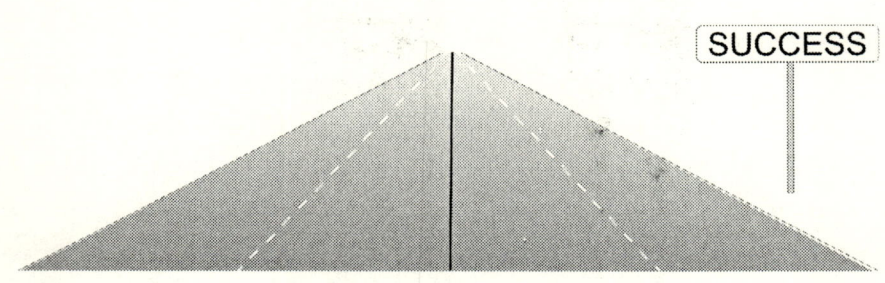

1
Introduction to Success

There are no secrets to success. It is the result of preparation, hard work, and learning from failure.
Colin Powell, Former U.S. Secretary of State

Every one of us has dreams of acquiring more money, enjoying better health, practicing good habits, having a wonderful relationship with our partner, overcoming limiting beliefs, and developing a stronger personality and skills for a happier life. In fact, we had considerably more dreams when we were kids, and some of these start to diminish with the daily obstacles and problems we experience in life.

Somewhere deep inside us we develop many limiting beliefs, habits, and behaviors. Our goals either change as a result or, in some cases, disappear altogether. We replace our goals with smaller or simpler goals to keep going, and that is not the right CHOICE!

The best way to predict your future is to create the right future that meets your dreams. Basically, you will become what you think about most of the time. Let me explain this in one simple example. If you think about a college degree, and work very hard to achieve the required score to join the right university that offers that degree and search about the possible jobs you might get with this degree. Further more, if you look for people who completed this degree and consult with them the pros and cons of pursuing the study of this degree and the associated possible jobs after graduating, then this becomes what you think about most of the time. You are creating a visual picture of your target, and now this will prepare you to go thru the different challenges to acquire this degree. There is a higher chance that you will achieve this degree in comparison of another person who does not even dream of that. My point is that you should not leave any objective vague or unclear. It is very crucial that you find out what you really want, and think about what it takes to get it. The basic model of getting what you want can be summarized as explained on the following steps which will guarantee a fast-track success:

- Clearly determine what your goals are.

- Prioritize them, and then tackle them.

Have a crystal clear vision of what you really want to achieve.

It is important to set goals that you really want to achieve. Do not climb the wrong mountain. Once you reach the wrong peak, you will see that it is not your vision. Setting goals you want to achieve saves you energy, time, and money. Clarity of goals eliminates confusion about your vision of the future. Once again and as I mentioned about the college degree example earlier, I have personally met many people who graduated from college with the wrong major. They carry this action to their jobs and, eventually, to their lives and future. Spend enough time in determining what you really want, as this step will help you focus on your actions and behaviors.

Organize and prioritize your goals; then tackle them one by one.

Goal setting is an important step that you need to take now and immediately. A study of a group of college seniors at an American university illustrates these points. A group of students was asked if they had dreams and goals and if they had a clear vision about how and when to achieve them. After fifteen years, the study followed up on the same group of students to see their progress with their goals. An amazing 97 percent of students who achieved their goals were clear about what they wanted to achieve. They wrote their goals down during an early stage of their lives. Only 3 percent of the sample managed to achieve their goals without having a clear plan and strategy. I am sure that you would prefer to have the higher odds of 97 percent, so you need to follow their way.

One suggested strategy

The following model is useful in achieving your goals. It can be modified according to the nature of your goals.

1. List all your goals and assign a date of completion.

2. Divide your goals into three main categories—one-year goals, five-year goals, and ten-year goals.

3. Prioritize the goals within each category by classifying them as extremely important, very important, important, and least important. One possible classification might be the different dimensions of your life, e.g., Health, Career, Financial, Spiritual, Social, Relationship, etc.

4. Write down a step-by-step plan for each goal within each category and have a clear strategy on how to achieve each one of them.

5. Use the law of attraction, discussed in chapter 5, to expedite your progress toward these goals.

6. Every three months, choose one day to review your master list and the three categories. Never break this schedule. I suggest a day during the first week of each quarter (e.g., January 2, April 4, and so on).

I have supplied you with three generic forms for each category in Appendix D. Do not be confused with step six above and the tables in Appendix D. Step six is a general suggestion for periodic review that will energize you and make you ready for the more specific review, as illustrated in Appendix D.

Summary Points and Insight of Chapter 1:

- Every dream you had or you have right now is achievable.

- Everyone is a unique person who can develop a way of creating a defined future.

- Thoughts determine your destiny through the actions and decisions you make.

- It is possible for you to change yourself, and that is only possible if you change the way you think.

- Success is not limited to anyone; you can have it if you decide that is what you want.

- You will always get what you expect.

- Set your one-year, five-year, and ten-year goals and monitor your progress.

2
The Law of Quantum Physics

The empires of the future are the empires of the mind.
Winston Churchill, Former Prime Minister of England (1874–1965)

It is a fact in physics that everything in this universe falls into discrete and indivisible units of energy called quanta. The basic component of all material things is energy. Furthermore, our imagination, sound, feelings, and thoughts are all energies with a specific frequency that correspond to the nature of the item. This energy has two behaviors in quantum physics, wave and particle.

Furthermore, similar energies [which have similar frequencies] attract each other since they resonate with each other. This can be easily seen if you place two pianos in a quiet room and you press the third key from the right, the second piano will absorb this energy on the same key on its keyboard and will resonate and vibrate at the same time. It is amazing how like things attract each other.

This concept is applicable in everything that we think of or do as everything is simply energy in accordance to the law of quantum physics. You should watch what you are vibrating and then consequently what you are attracting. It is your choice and focus that will determine your destiny, whether it is good luck and happiness or poverty and sadness. By holding pleasant thoughts and by creating a positive image of our success, you will attract more of that and you will reach and achieve that. On the other hand, by holding bad thoughts about the future and destiny, you will resonate with an energy that brings about bad results.

As a result, you have to be very careful about your thoughts, as they become your present and, eventually, your future. If you want to choose your future, just choose it now and relate to the supporting ideas—not opposite or conflicting ideas to achieve your future goals. This universal law does not have exceptions or special cases; it is applied to you and me—and to everything in the universe. You get what you think of and expect to receive most of the time. In case this does not happen, then you might have another conflicting belief that keeps you on hold from achieving your goal. For example, if you think about having a healthy body, and you tried to know everything about how practicing a sport benefits your body but you have a limiting belief that you are too old to practice any sport, then most likely you will not have a healthy body.

You should eliminate any belief that stops you from creating the right resonance. You should in this case, for example, replace that belief with another empowering belief like, yes, I can play so many sports even if I am not that young. There are people out there who practice sport at different age categories. Hence, there must be so many good sports for me to choose from. This will help you to resonate the right sport and see it possible.

To help you best utilize law of quantum physics, I devoted the next chapter to explore positive thinking basics and then I followed that by two chapters to talk about the law of attraction and how to activate it in your favor. Positive thinking and the law of attraction is the fruit that we obtain from quantum physics when you apply it properly.

The book shows you how your thoughts formulate your actions and then how your actions shape your personality. Your personality then decides your destiny, so you must choose the right kind of thoughts that you hold in your mind frequently. It is very simple to create your future if you alter your thoughts appropriately.

Summary Points and Insight of Chapter 2:

- Quantum physics is a fact that combines similar energies with a specific frequency, which is the way God created the universe.

- There is no one exempted from the influence of quantum physics in the universe.

- Be careful of your thoughts; positive thinking yields positive results, and the converse is true, too.

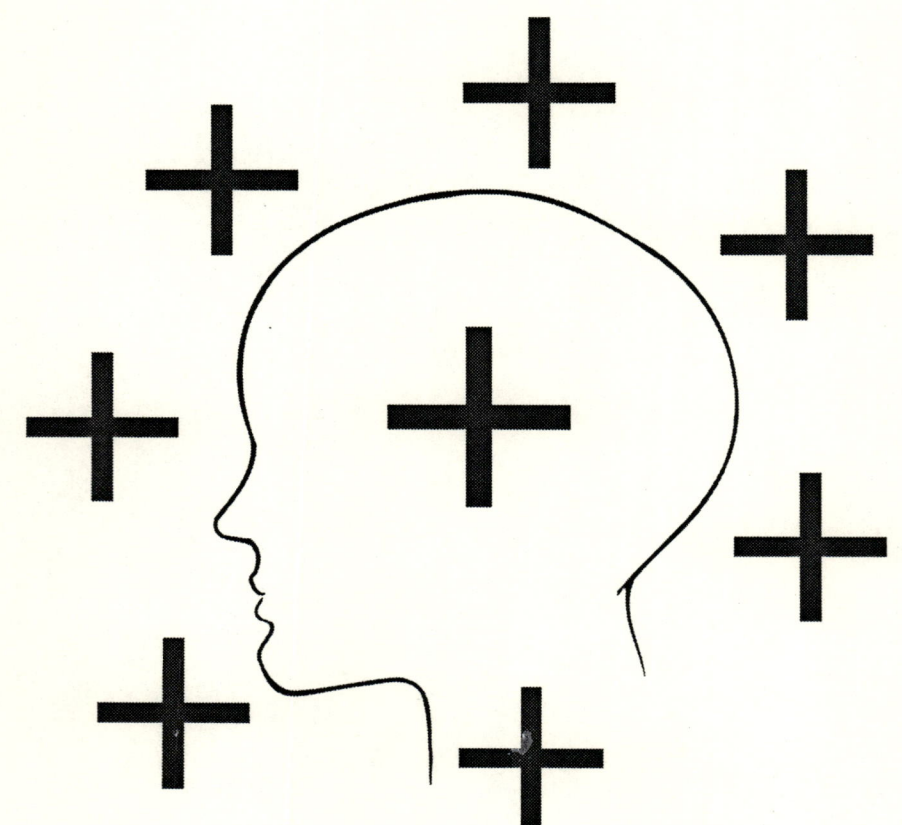

3
Positive Thinking Power

In the middle of difficulty lies opportunity.
Albert Einstein (1879–1955)

Every idea, thought, action, and feeling requires a thinking process. This process can then follow a negative interpretation or a positive one. In fact, it is our choice to project any idea on the positive side or the negative side.

When we project the idea on the positive plane of the world, we create positive energy with a certain frequency and release it into the universe. It eventually reflects back a positive energy of an equal amount and same frequency. In this process, we have a positive sequence of thoughts, actions, and, finally, destinations. When you hold negative energy and choose not to release it, and you go beyond that and replace it with a positive energy [idea or thought] then you will transform that into positive energy, and you will create a positive attitude and character within yourself.

The opposite is also true. When you choose to project and interpret an idea on the negative plane of the world, you will create a negative energy in the universe. Certainly, the reflection will be from the same nature on the quantity and frequency. You will be dragged into negative actions, and then it means ultimately that you have chosen an undesirable destination.

Furthermore, the matter amplifies according to the law of quantum physics. As positive energies and reflections attract more positive energy, negative energies lead to more negative results and bad outcomes. The way you think and how you act on it literally becomes your present and future. If you want happiness, then you can have it now by choosing happiness and nothing else!

Summary Points and Insight of Chapter 3:

- Positive thinking conserves your power and helps you concentrate on high-value goals.

- The universe always works for you if you decide and think positively.

- Develop the required set of skills with the appropriate strategies to achieve your goals.

- Be committed and responsible to take the charge of your life now.

4
Keep in Mind These Universal Laws

Those who cannot change their minds cannot change anything.
George Bernard Shaw (1856–1950)

In previous chapters, we see how the law of quantum physics explains the relationship between similar energies and their frequencies and how they work. It is amazing how like things resonate with each other. We have seen also how this law applies its power on ideas, thoughts, feelings, sounds, images, and actions. It is a large domain of energies and frequencies that covers everything in our universe.

To get the most out of the law of quantum physics, we discussed positive thinking theory and how it has a dominant effect on our energy conservation and transformation. When you develop a positive attitude and character toward various life challenges, you will benefit in your journey of this life. This will be achieved by activating the law of quantum physics to attract similar positive energies. We will attract prosperity and love by looking at the half-full glass and starting each day with the motivation and courage to reach for our future. You can create your own future if you act in your present moment. It has been said that time has three windows; namely, the past, present, and future. You can learn from your past experiences and act and execute your plans in the present, creating your own future that you would like to have.

There are several universal laws that govern all different aspects of our life. I have found it crucial to mention the one related to the subject of this book. I will describe those laws concisely so you can benefit and keep them in mind at all times.

The law of cause and effect

This is a very important law we experience in our life. Nothing happens by chance. Every action we take has a specific outcome associated with it. Every time we take a particular action with the same set of conditions, we get the same outcome. For example, you might say that you tried to have good relations with others, but you fail all the time. This indicates that the wrong approach is being followed over and over again. You would need to change your action in this case if you want to seek a different result. No matter how many times you do that very action, do not expect a different outcome. It is only possible to change your action and behavior to have a different outcome and result.

The law of correspondence

This law derives from the global energy theory. The whole universe is a big domain of energies and frequencies of which we are part. This law is analogous to the echo phenomena where whatever we say returns to us with the same meaning and a similar voice. When we act positively, we send a positive energy into this domain at a certain frequency. The global energy and its domain reflect the same amount of energy within that specific frequency. If we help someone who asks for help, we will find someone who will help if we ask. However, if we committed some bad action to a person at a time, this will reflect from the universe. Another person will commit a bad action directed at us at another time. The global domain of energy governs everything, so be careful of what you are sending into this universe because it will come back again.

The law of the subconscious mind

This law explains how the subconscious mind perceives things. Whatever reaches the subconscious mind on the learning mode will be believed. The subconscious mind does not differentiate between real life and the imagination. This factor could be tremendously limiting when a person fears something that does not exist or thinks he does not have the capability needed for a skill or action. However, if you deploy positive programming, then your subconscious mind should believe you are capable of doing certain things and ignore your limiting beliefs. This law is explained well in the science of neuro-linguistic programming (NLP). NLP is a very effective method and is described in a different chapter of this book. For now, just note that you need to program yourself positively.

The law of equivalent thinking

The minute our brain starts thinking about something, similar ideas pop up. The more time you spend on this activity, the more you will associate different but similar ideas. For example, when you think about a bad incident that happened to you in the past, your brain opens similar mental files. You start remembering every similar incident, and then you start to feel bad. The same thing holds true when you think of your loved ones; your brain will remind you of your loved ones and the good memories associated with those people as well.

The law of concentration

Once our brain thinks about a particular subject or item, it will observe it everywhere. How many times have you decided to buy an item and then, suddenly, you see an advertisement about it on television, hear something about it from a friend, and see many shops offer it? It becomes popular wherever you go. Where was this item before? It was not in your focus then, but now it is, and that is why you see it a lot.

The law of expectation

With this law, you get what you expect. It works like a magnet where your expectation comes true. Once again, you have to be very careful about what you expect.

Summary Points and Insight of Chapter 4:

- There are universal laws that organize our life, and everyone obeys these laws whether they choose to do so or not.

- The law of cause and effect states that everything happens for a reason. Nothing comes from nothing.

- The law of correspondence states that the universe will work as a mirror that returns energy in the opposite direction and, in particular, toward the sender with same amount of energy.

- The law of the subconscious mind states that your subconscious does not differentiate between reality and imagination.

- The law of equivalent thinking brings similar ideas into your thinking. You amplify those ideas and increase your understanding and experience of that particular idea.

- The law of concentration spreads your perception to capture anything related to your focus.

- The law of expectation works for you or against you, so pay enough attention to what you expect.

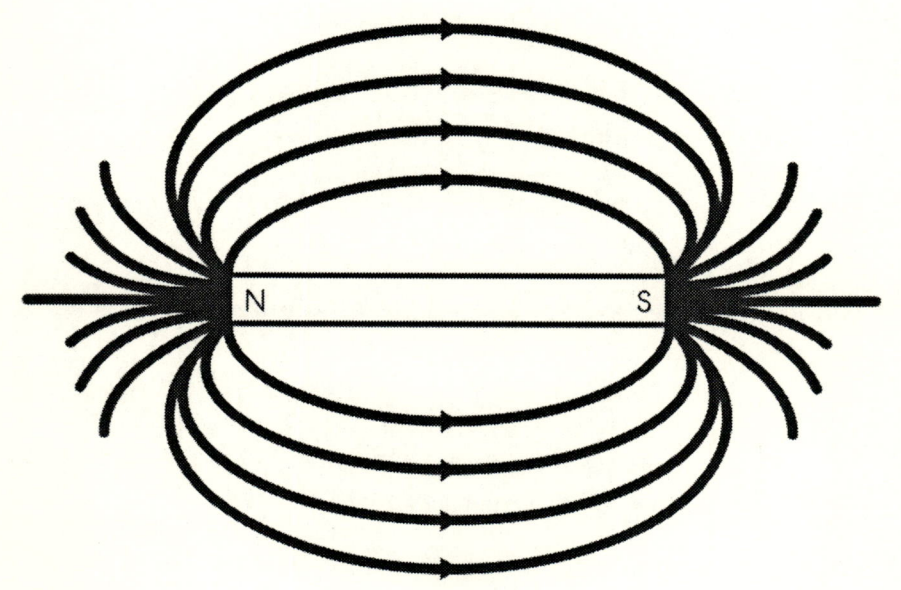

5
The Law of Attraction

The greatest discovery of my generation is that human beings can alter their lives by altering their attitudes of mind.
William James (1842–1910)

In the first four chapters, we develop an understanding of how success is possible for everyone. We also see how quantum physics explains that like things attract each other. In this chapter, we discuss a quick method to cause this attraction to work on our desired goal by activating the law of attraction.

All of us practice the law of attraction without knowing it. This program has been customized to make this law work for you instead of working against you. If you expect something to go wrong, it will. The power of expectation lies at the heart of the meaning of the law of attraction.

In fact, to gain the most out of theories of quantum physics—universal laws, positive thinking, focus, and concentration are well integrated to come up with within this new technique. The law of attraction works for you and takes you to your destiny in no time. The minute you start practicing the simple exercises for only three weeks, you will feel a major shift in your life; you will feel that you can achieve the impossible. You will boost happiness in your life and even beyond that when you start attracting the good fortune in all dimensions of your life. This law will offer you the secret of making your dreamed desires come immediately true and only in three weeks.

It is true that each goal has a pattern that consists of a sequence of events that starts by initiating a thought that triggers and determines your words, affecting the kind of actions you take. These actions will be aligned with your deeply buried thoughts that represent your dreams and desires. Those actions will take you to your destiny and will convert your thoughts into real achievement of your goals.

To facilitate this activation, I broke this law into four possible aspects of success. The four aspects are wealth, health, love, and luck. This division provides more depth of the subject. However, the explanations here can be similarly applied to other aspects of your life and goals. After the explanation of these four divisions, I will show you how to activate this law the minute you decide on your goal.

The law of attraction for wealth

Start depositing a fixed amount of money every month in a separate account that you never touch. For example, you need to start by setting aside 10 percent of your salary and seek to move to a higher percentage as you move forward. On your next increase, do not forget to allocate an additional saving from this increase. Keep this strategy for every increase in your income from this moment onward. This accumulation of money will attract more money to you, and you will meet your financial target at an amazing speed. You will have a life free from worries about your financial independence.

Think the rich way when you spend money. All rich people know what they should spend on and when they should spend it. It is hard to grow your money and very easy to lose it.

Think about a financial goal and set a deadline to achieve it. I will show you how to trigger this in your mindset later in this chapter using a three-step program.

Make a logbook where you document all expenditures. Having done that, examine how you spend money and on which items you spend most. Find out what was really needed, and what was a waste of your money. Eliminate wasteful expenditures in the future and make better decisions on your future purchases.

Help others achieve their financial goals, as this will benefit you through the law of correspondence. Also, you will learn a lot about the process of making money and how others make money in this world of opportunity.

Observe how your salary has grown from the first day you were employed until now, and see how your expenses increased correspondingly. This is a usual behavior, and it is guaranteed to make you suffer financially as you progress in this life. Take the lead and stop this behavior immediately. At your next increase, start saving 25 percent and move fast to 50 percent per month of the amount of the increase. This technique by itself will develop your ability to have a large account and the mentality of the rich in a very short period of time.

Remember the law of abundance in this life: there is a whole lot of money out there, and you need to rest assured that you can get as much—and everyone can get as much—as you want from this infinite wealth in the universe.

The law of attraction for health

This aspect of law of attraction is the single most important thing you should put on your list of objectives. In fact, health of the brain and body are tied together. A good healthy brain will provide a healthy productive body, which will enable you to have a happy, energetic life.

The healthier life you have, the less you will need to spend from your account and wealth. This benefits you further by saving you time instead of being sick and wasting time in trips to seek medical treatment. You will avoid spending on medicine and the huge depression that illness might cause.

Organize your day and night so that you have a schedule to follow. This will positively impact your lifestyle and give your time a much higher value. The time you waste will never come again, so be careful about this gift and how you consume it. Time is like a bank account; you should withdraw only what you really need, so you should utilize your time and take full advantage of every minute to move closer toward your objectives and goals.

Make a regular time to visit the gym and have friends who encourage you to go. You will eventually develop a fit, healthy body. This time should be at least three hours per week. I've found it very useful to have thirty minutes of exercise on a daily basis as an alternative program. Physical exercise reduces stress and circulates blood. You will enjoy a clean breath every time you exercise.

Visit your doctor and see what kind of food you should eat and what type of drinks you should have. Also describe your most consumed items to determine if those choices are healthy or if you should seek alternatives.

If you are smoking, quit this bad habit immediately. It is one factor that might cause diseases and health problems. In fact, smoking might cause death in the long run. Besides it is a waste of money. Smoking will limit your choices when you sit with your family and friends, take transportation, or eat in a restaurant. Smoking also makes your clothes and body smell bad. You become a slave to the addiction after a relatively short period of time. It serves as a bad example for your children, and I am sure you do not want them to smoke in the future.

Another major problem is alcohol consumption. Drinking alcohol has been a major cause for many wealth, health, and social problems. It reduces your ability to focus and concentrate. It will eat your money and time very quickly and unnoticeably. Replace alcoholic beverages with fresh juices and healthy drinks. Drink lots of water as experts indicate that water might help us recover from so many health difficulties. It is a major component of our bodies after all, and our bodies need enough of this resource.

Another good habit is breathing the right way. Most people breathe short, fast, and shallow breaths that do not provide enough oxygen for the body. Your lungs become very congested. You need to take long, deep breaths to enrich your body with the required oxygen. Advanced techniques of breathing are taught in yoga and other sports. You can check with a consultant in this field, and you will appreciate your active body immediately within few days of doing this. Take at least ten long, deep breaths in the morning, at midday, and during the evening.

Make it a daily habit to practice some sports and join some sports club for weekends.

The law of attraction for love

Love is an immeasurable thing that grows forever. It embraces us with a peaceful dynamic emotion once we experience it. True love is the best thing you can ever get in this life; it turns the impossible to the possible. It is that miracle that was given to us so that we have meaning for ourselves and the universe around us. God created love and gave it to us.

You need to love others to gain their love. This is the only secret formula of love.

Get closer to your parents, see what makes them happy, and do those things for them. Send them a present from time to time to let them know that you remember them. Visit them and call them as you start to have your own life and your own family. Do not forget your brothers and sisters.

The reason I started with parents and siblings is that they represent your initial family members. You need to energize your love and renew it with your spouse and children, too.

Make some time for your spouse and children every single day and put it on your daily schedule as a priority to see what they need and how they lived their day. Make a special time to go out with them for a dinner in a good restaurant. Arrange for a picnic every month with your family, and spend the full day with them. Have fun with them.

Remember the effect of gifts on your family and surprise them with at least simple and not very costly items, as this will make them happy. They will love you more. Bring flowers occasionally to introduce romance again in your marriage.

Keep in touch with your friends, and use kind words when you speak with people. These words reflect outward to others about how you feel about life and what kind of experiences you have encountered thus far. Avoid talking badly about people, as this will encourage them to talk badly about you. Do not spread rumors if it is untrue; this will degrade others' ability to trust you. Learn how to forgive others for their mistakes. This, by itself, will conserve your energy that otherwise would be consumed with hatred toward others. Replace hate with love, and you will live differently. You will see a brighter color, and you will look from a wider window onto life.

The law of attraction for luck

It is common to say certain people are lucky. Similarly, there are people whom we would describe as unlucky; they always miss opportunities. Is there something really called "luck," and what exactly is it? In our general understanding, if someone has a resource or skill that is well suited when an opportunity arises, then that person is lucky. But what makes those "lucky" people have luck, and why are they blessed?

Lucky people always feel that they are special, and they work hard and strive for an opportunity before it becomes available. The old saying "be ready for the opportunity so that when it comes you can get it" means that luck requires preparation and makes taking advantage of the opportunity easier when it presents itself.

We have seen many people who think that they are unlucky, but actually they never work toward those opportunities. They send negative energy into the universe; and again, according to the law of correspondence, the universe replies in kind with bad luck—just as they expected.

To have a better luck, you must have a positive expectation about your future and its possibilities. Avoid the energy-suckers who tell you how bad the future is and how much you are limited by your abilities and resources. They just see the dark side. The sky is always cloudy for them, and they believe that they do not have the luxury of making choices in this life. You have to be confident that you are unique in this universe, that there is only one person like you. This person is you.

Remember that the outer world is just a reflection of your inner world. If you want the outer world to send you luck and success, feel that and program it in yourself. Charge yourself with the good memories and how many times you were surprised by your luck in the past. It is definitely possible to have that again and again. Visualize your future with beautiful pictures in every aspect. Visualize your dream home, the car of your dreams, and a wonderful family. Replace any ugly pictures and negative images in your brain with positive ones that reduce your chance of bad luck dramatically.

Set your family at the highest level of priority, and make them feel they are lucky. This behavior will have a very positive impact on your life. You will feel you are surrounded with people who care about you and who are willing to do anything for you to be a fortunate person.

Socialize with friends who have positive attitudes, dreams, and goals. Look forward to this life and expect the best to come. Remember your past and how many times you imagined something good would happen for you and it did happen.

Apply the three-step exercise to activate the law of attraction to work for you, as described later in this book. List your goals and find out what you need to have to realize them. All of this will make you a luckier person as you achieve and acquire more success.

Real-life examples of the law of attraction

Many stories and cases illustrate the law of attraction. I would like to give you some real-life examples from people who applied the law of attraction and got what they wanted. I will follow that section with specific procedures on how to activate the law of attraction to work for you.

Waiting list for accommodations at the company residence

This is a story of a friend who moved recently to the city. He was struggling to find a house to rent in the company-owned housing complex. Company employees usually had to wait a few years, and there was no exception to the waiting policy.

I was chatting with this friend, and he conveyed to me his difficulty just to share with me. I told him about the law of attraction, and he rejected the idea completely at the beginning. I assured him that it would only take a few minutes every day and that he would lose nothing, so why not give it a shot. The man promised me that he would try. Just after a few days, he called me to say that the housing unit had called him to tell him that there were a few houses in which he could stay. But there was a lottery. If he won, he would only have to wait for about sixty days for a renovation of the house. My friend accepted that. A few days later, they called him again and told him that his name had been selected. It is an unbelievable story, but it worked out.

Career promotion after frustration

This man's situation was full of worries, and even his work condition was very limited in scope for the future. Once he applied the law of attraction, several changes happened to him during the first week about the way he thought. This change triggered his colleagues' and bosses' attention, and he was promoted. He started to work much harder than before. It worked again, and it will work again every time. I guarantee it.

Huge deposit then a fat bank account

This is a true story about another friend who had been struggling financially for a long time. He applied the law of attraction to activate wealth. A few days later, he made a decision to open a new bank account just to set some money aside. Within a few months, he started to accumulate money, and he was able to close all open financial commitments. Now, he started to think in multiple investment opportunities. His life changed as his mind started to look at money differently. Recently, I know he started to build a fat bank account!

There are so many other examples that show how people have attracted health and luck in their lives just by deploying this law, and I have included just a few.

I am not saying that the law of attraction will change real life magically while you sit idle but it will make you attract good actions and will change the way you think about your situation. You will make better decisions, too. It is tightly related to the law of equivalent thinking of the subconscious mind. This is the energy you will send to the universe and you receive in reply on your new behavior immediately.

Summary Points and Insight of Chapter 5:

- Law of attraction extracts its concept from the law of quantum physics; where we attract what we think about most of the time.

- Wealth, health, love, and luck are just four examples of where success can be achieved. You can apply similar procedures for other goals.

- The law of attraction is extremely powerful to get you what you want once you start using it.

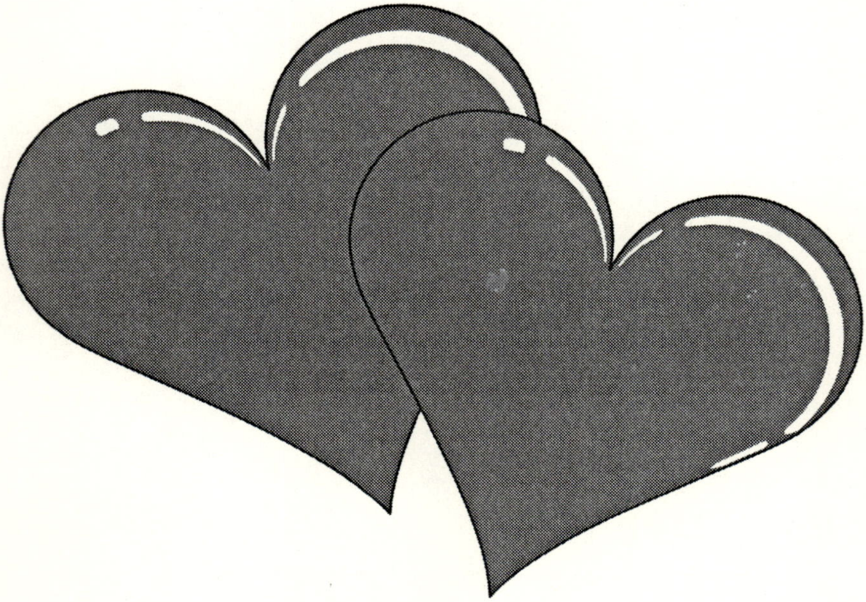

6
Activating the Law of Attraction

If you can imagine it, you can achieve it; if you can dream it, you can become it.
William Arthur Ward

Our focus here is to activate the law of attraction to work for your desired goals. It will establish a tunnel between your thoughts and your goals. I will show you how to build that tunnel between your thoughts and your goals and how to move through this tunnel toward your goal. Your desired goal is at the end of the tunnel.

The following diagram simplifies this process for you:

Thoughts——Law of Attraction——Your Goals

The law of attraction brings your thoughts and goals together, and you will become what you think about most. It will make you think about resources, ideas, and shortcuts to get to your goal very quickly. It will attract the similar energies to vibrate with your thoughts and actions.

The procedure has been broken into the following three steps. Each step has to be completed within a certain period of time. Furthermore, each step has one exercise that will be described in detail.

You must commit to follow the three steps according to the schedule mentioned below.

Step 1

This first step should start on the first day and continue for twenty-one days. You need to complete exercise one on a daily basis during these twenty-one days.

Step 2

The second step begins on the eighth day of step one and continues for the following fourteen days. You will need to complete exercise two on a daily basis during these fourteen days.

Step 3

The last step starts on day number fifteen from the beginning of step one and continues for the following seven days. You will need to complete exercise three on a daily basis for seven days.

Your success in activating the law of attraction depends heavily on your commitment to completing the three steps without any procrastination. It is guaranteed to have a tremendous effect on achieving your goals in a way that you have never dreamed of.

We will go through each step with its own exercise in detail in order to simplify the process with minimal effort.

A Very Important Note to Keep in Mind

While you practice the program, no one should know about it. You can only inform others after you achieve your goal. This concept is essential for the success of the three different steps and the three exercises. This helps you contain your energy within yourself so that your thoughts have a better focus. Then you keep your concentration crystal clear. Some people might distract you or discourage you, and then this will work against you. Be cautious.

Step 1

You will need to do this exercise for twenty-one days.

Exercise 1

This exercise is broken into two parts.

Part A. Write your goal in a clear, short, and powerful statement as if you have already achieved it.

If your goal is to attract something like having a closer relationship with your partner, then your statement could be: "I have a wonderful and lovely relationship with my partner now."

If your goal is to acquire a certain amount of money, then your statement could be the following: "I have a hundred thousand dollars in my account now."

For a career goal, your statement could be:

- I am an expert in computer networking technology;
- I am the head of my department now; or
- I am an outstanding employee now.

On the other hand, if your goal is to repel something away like weight reduction, then you need to make your statement sound positive. You could write:

- I have a fit and healthy body now.

Or if your goal were to quit smoking, then you would write: I am enjoying deep breathing and excellent health now.

Part B. Now that you have written your goal in a clear, short, and powerful statement, you need to have a small notebook of at least twenty-one pages. For each day for the next three weeks, you write the page number and the date. Then write your statement twenty-one times on the page. This will have to be done daily during the three weeks.

See Appendix A for sample forms for exercise 1.

Step 2

You should have been completing exercise one during the previous seven days when you start exercise two, which covers days eight through twenty-one.

Exercise 2: (Establishing the Tunnel Experience)

In this exercise, I will move you from your thought to your goal through the tunnel we mentioned earlier. This exercise will take one minute every day. It is broken into two parts as well.

Part A. Each morning before you leave your home, sit in a comfortable place in your home. First, close your eyes and start to disconnect from the world around you. (Just count backward from fifteen slowly.) This process should take about fifteen seconds.

Part B. After fifteen seconds, start imagining yourself as if you have already achieved your goal and you are enjoying the fine details of it (smell, color, touch, luxury, emotions, etc.). Continue this exercise for forty-five seconds.

    This exercise should start in week two and continue for fourteen mornings on a daily basis. This exercise helps reduce the distance between your thoughts and your goals. You will see an amazing improvement toward getting your goal in hands.

Check Appendix B for a sample form for exercise two.

Step 3

You should have been completing exercise one daily for the previous fourteen days and exercise two seven days before starting exercise three. Exercise three covers day fifteen to day twenty-one.

Exercise 3: (Goal Achievement Appreciation)

In this exercise, you become part of the law of attraction function. You need to recognize and appreciate every small and large sign toward your goal achievement. This exercise takes one minute every night. It is broken into two parts.

Part A. Once you are at home and before you go to bed, do a similar thing to exercise 2 but without going into your thoughts. First, close your eyes and start the connect part. (Just count backward from fifteen slowly.) This process should take about fifteen seconds.

Part B. Start to appreciate any small or large step toward your goal, and then follow that by imagining that you have already achieved your goal with its details. Do this for forty-five seconds. You will have to do this exercise on daily basis during the third week of this program.

Check Appendix C for a sample form for exercise three.

The previous chapters discuss success and achievement and review some relevant universal laws and the mechanism of the subconscious mind. This chapter provides a review of the theory of the law of attraction. Finally, we used those concepts to activate the law of attraction as you have seen in this chapter.

Our focus so far has been on the emotions, thoughts, and actions. The next chapter explores access to our brain and how to go beyond that to program ourselves to be effective, successful people in taking the right actions with the right and optimal strategies.

Summary Points and Insight of Chapter 6:

- You need to commit to the three exercises for twenty-one days. You will see a major shift in your thinking, and you will take serious steps toward your goals.

- If you miss one day of the exercises, you need to start over again for another twenty-one days to activate the law of attraction effectively.

- Sample forms have been supplied for exercises one, two, and three.

- Sample statements have been supplied for different goals at the end of the book in the appendices.

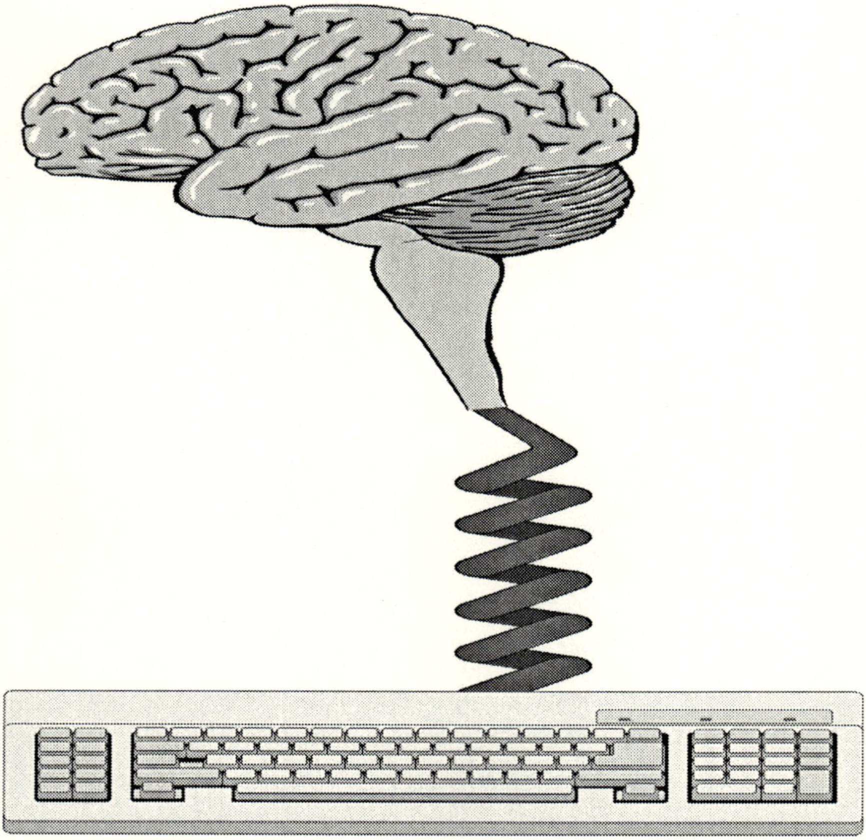

7

Control Your Own Life with NLP

Change is the law of life. And those who look only to the past or present are certain to miss the future.
John Fitzgerald Kennedy (1917–1963)

In the early seventies, neuro-linguistic programming (NLP) was discovered as a result of an in-depth study about behavioral modeling of human success. The initial contribution to the development of NLP was done by John Grinder, who studied linguistics and received his PhD from the University of California, San Diego, and Richard Bandler, a mathematician. Their study of how successful people achieved success, managed to have control over their lives, and clear obstacles created this course of science. NLP deals with higher achievement and the required strategies for that success.

Each word or root of NLP or neuro-linguistic programming serves as a pillar of this science. "Neuro" is the association between our body and mind, where it functions through the nervous system and our body's five senses, through which we communicate information to our brain to store, compare, process, and react.

The second word, "linguistic," refers to the representation system of communication, verbal or nonverbal. The nonverbal includes facial expression, body movement, and so forth. NLP extracts its power from reading these codes and sending the right reply to the same form (e.g., to facial expressions and body movement).

The last part, "programming," refers to the required techniques and strategies to alter the nervous system, verbal language, and nonverbal language to achieve our desired goals.

The map and the territory

If you have a map of the city, you still do not have the city. At the same time, the city is not the map. To further complicate things, everyone has his own different map of the city that he or she uses to navigate through streets.

This situation is analogous to our real-life situations: everyone has an individual perception of any situation in life. This perception limits the features and the resources of the situation. If you view a certain goal as unachievable or impossible, then it is most likely because your map of this goal and the road to acquire it are so much limited in its resources and options. You will develop your own strategy in seeking your goal based on your own perception. It might be the most difficult strategy or methodology. NLP advises you to widen your perception to see how others managed to succeed in reaching the same goal.

The belief system

If you say you cannot do something, then you really cannot do that particular thing. However, if you believe that you can do a certain action and achieve a certain goal, then you can. What is the truth about the situation here?

Your mind and body are tied together to provide you with what you want. Your belief about yourself will shape and determine your resources. Your mind and body will follow your belief system on whatever way you imagine yourself.

I remember one friend who was addicted to coffee. If he did not have his cup of coffee in the morning, he would get a headache until he had his daily brew. He believed he was a slave for caffeine. One day, he passed by my office and I offered him decaffeinated coffee unintentionally. He went with me to attend a meeting. By lunch time, he mentioned that if he did not drink coffee in the morning, he would have a headache because of the amount of caffeine he needed to consume every day.

I asked him, "Did you have coffee today?"

He said, "Yes, you offered me some, and that is why I have no headache."

I told him it was decaffeinated.

He screamed, "Oh, no, that is why I felt a little bit of a headache."

In fact, a few minutes later, he started to feel a strong headache.

What happened here is that his belief system triggered his headache. This is a true story, and I am sure you have encountered similar stories for something or another.

Whatever you believe about yourself and your ability, then your mind will adapt itself and goes further to change your physiology to meet that belief. The change you want in your life starts with changing your beliefs.

Metaphor and the own belief system

Our notion about things determines how we feel toward them and whether we can acquire them. If you imagine that studying for a medical degree resembles carrying ten books on your shoulders every year, you end up adding ten books more on your shoulders until you graduate. This image creates an upsetting picture in your mind, and you feel the pain in your shoulders. You give up studying medicine. The metaphor you created for studying medicine and achieving this degree made it impossible for you to get there.

However, if you imagine that by enrolling in the medical school and going through the program, then you will gradually become more knowledgeable in the field, then you are creating a good metaphor for studying medicine and achieving your goal. This way, you will see that the field will be introduced to you in small pieces every year, and you will have the luxury of seeing real-life cases. You will absorb the required knowledge as you move on in your college studies. You will also imagine how proud you will be to serve others by treating them. You might invent something for humanity. You will be a very distinct and appreciated member of the community and society as everyone respects a qualified doctor. You will have the opportunity to expand your knowledge and be specialized on a highly sophisticated area of science and medicine. Even financially, a good doctor is paid well.

Do you see the difference between the two metaphors? The first one discourages you and makes you give up. The second one, on the other hand, creates a tremendous power within you to take the challenge and study more hours and seek a brighter future. However you associate your imagination with how you achieve your goal, you will have a major impact on your choices, decisions, and then your actions.

Visual, auditory, and kinesthetic learning styles and representational systems

Everyone uses his five senses to discover his surroundings. At the same time, some senses have a dominant effect of perception and response than others. To simplify the analysis of this, NLP classifies personalities into three possible types. The first type is the visual personality, where the person draws a picture of what he thinks and how he interprets things. This personality relies more on the visual sensory system. These people tend to be fast and see the overall picture of a situation. They tend not to care much about the details. Certain words like "see," "watch," and "appear" attract this personality. The visual sensory system is naturally used to perceive and interpret real-life situations.

The second type is the auditory personality, where the person communicates more efficiently through the hearing sensory system. Certain words like "hear," "listen," and "sound like" attract this personality and are easy to perceive. The auditory sensory system is the main tool for perception here.

The third type is the kinesthetic personality, where the person feels situations more than sees or hears them. It is a slow or a deep personality where the person cares about the touch of the thing and how it feels. The person is affected more by words like "feel," "touch," and "taste."

Each learning style is unique and works well if the other person has exactly the same personality type when they communicate with each other. However, everyone prefers one type out of the three. For example, a teacher might be a visual person, and one of his students might be an auditory person. This makes the communication very inefficient, difficult, and sometimes misleading.

A good question should now arise as to how we identify our own personality type and the people with whom we communicate.

Fortunately, NLP resolves this problem by analyzing verbal and nonverbal language.

Briefly, for the verbal language analysis and to find out what personality you are, observe what kind of words you use more when you describe a situation and what attracts you more—pictures, sounds, or the feeling of the thing itself. Again, for example, words like "see," "watch," and "view" would indicate that you are a visual type.

Another way to determine personality type is to observe the eye movement of the person talking to you. If the eye moves along a direct horizontal line, then this is related to an auditory sensory system. Once again, if this is dominant in the person talking to you, then he is most likely auditory type. However, if the eye moves downward from the direct horizontal lines, then this is related to the kinesthetic sensory system and then the person is most likely a kinesthetic type.

You cannot have a final judgment immediately; you need to observe this multiple times and in different situations to determine that very accurately. In fact, to establish a rapport with another person, NLP uses this kind of analysis to find out what type of personality you are talking to. Once this is determined, then choose the right style of communication with the other person according to his learning style.

Model success and then follow that model

There is an old saying that you do not need to reinvent the wheel. If you are looking to achieve a certain result and attain a certain goal, search for someone who has achieved that result and who has attained the same goal that you want. Analyze this person's behaviors and the way he thinks. Look into which qualities he used to get there. Find out how he developed those qualities. Set your plans to tackle them one at a time. Once you achieve these qualities, duplicate his behaviors exactly the same way that he did. From the law of cause and effect, you will get the same result that he got and you will achieve the same goal that he achieved.

Watch out for your state of mind and your behavior:

The way you respond to a certain situation might be totally different according to your state of mind. If you are relaxed and feeling great, you will usually make positive choices and decisions.

However, if you are tired and exhausted, you will have different responses to the same situation we talked about earlier. You might make the opposite decision as a rejection instead of acceptance and so forth.

One easy trick is to check a good memory of the past and visualize the whole situation of that memory. Try to remember the fine details of the memory. This will turn your focus; your state of mind will change gradually. Your decisions will be much more positive, and you will have better choices.

I want to stress the modeling portion of this chapter here. If you decide on a goal, search for someone who has achieved it in a way that you like. After you find that person, observe and mimic him in his strategy. You will eventually have the same outcome.

Summary Points and Insight of Chapter 7:

- NLP stands for neuro-linguistic programming.

- NLP relies on the nervous system, verbal and nonverbal language, and building a strategy for success.

- Your belief system determines how well you perceive the world outside and what is possible for you.

- You can duplicate others to achieve success if you model their strategies accurately and appropriately.

- You can change a behavior instantly using an anchor technique.

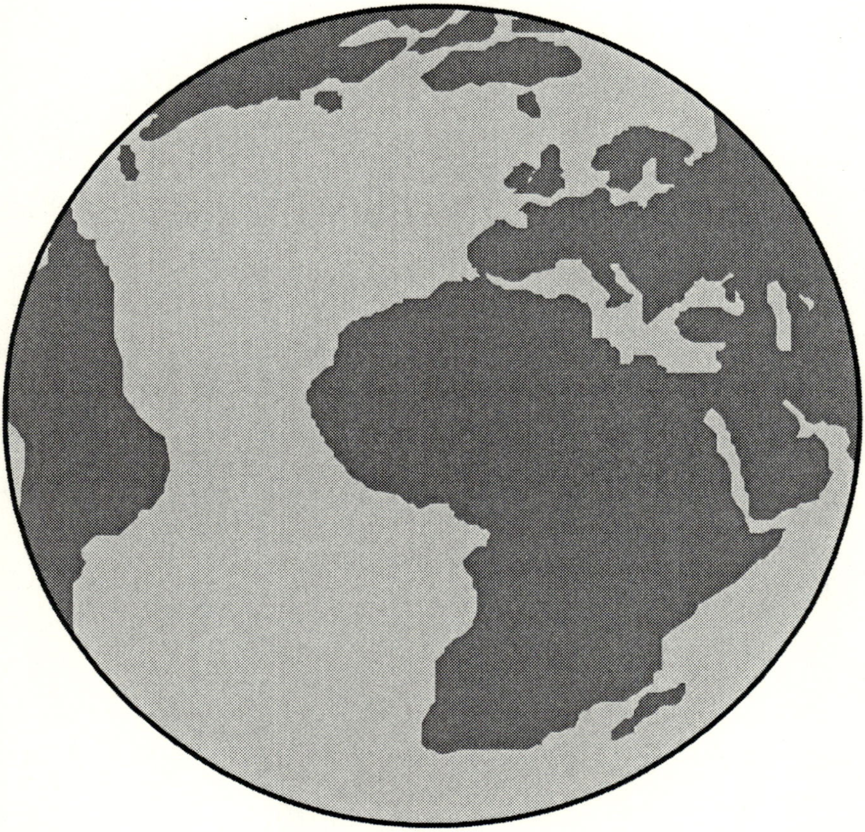

8
Be a Moving Success on the Globe

You are forgiven for your happiness and your successes only if you generously consent to share them.
Albert Camus (1913–1960)

As we started this book discussing success, I want you to develop the habit of sharing your success with others as well. It will make you a much more effective person and will enable you to see the bigger picture of success in your life. In fact, this will provide you with new ways to expand your experience as you will have the opportunity to learn from them as well. By acquiring the knowledge of controlling your feelings, beliefs, and thoughts, you can easily shape your future the way you want.

You will need to share your vision of the future with your family and the people you meet as well. You do not need to share your desired future car with a work colleague for example, although he might give you a one-million-dollar piece of advice that will help you make a better choice. Sometimes, sharing your vision will help you determine your timeline and required qualities more accurately.

Another piece of good advice is to discuss your strategies with the people you trust and who have experience in the field of your goal. Consulting with others might save you time and effort, and it could change your strategy completely to a better one. This way, you will be able to develop the optimal strategy suitable for your goal. You need to be persistent with your actions; you should not give up easily. This kind of commitment rewards you with high-quality results as you achieve your goals.

If you can have at least two mentors and coaches, you will see different aspects of your goals and the methodologies you use to acquire them. Many famous people, businessmen, and managers have coaches to keep them on track and to provide feedback as to their progress.

Keep in mind that your attitude is important. Have a personality that seeks the win-win-win approach. You should win, and the other side should win, too. Society should win or, at least, should not be hurt.

To be a moving success, you need to maintain a balance between the four aspects of success and beyond. You will enrich your life with highly challenging goals, and your personality will grow every day in different dimensions.

Remember that a person of high values and fixed principles will have self-respect and will gain respect from others as well. This person will build a strong character to face life's challenges and to attract life's opportunities as they come.

Summary Points and Insight of Chapter 8:

- Sharing success will enhance your relationships with others and increase your knowledge and experience.

- Having a mentor to monitor your progress and provide you with feedback will keep you on track toward your goals.

- Establishing a balance between different goals will shape a stronger person to face life's challenges as time goes by.

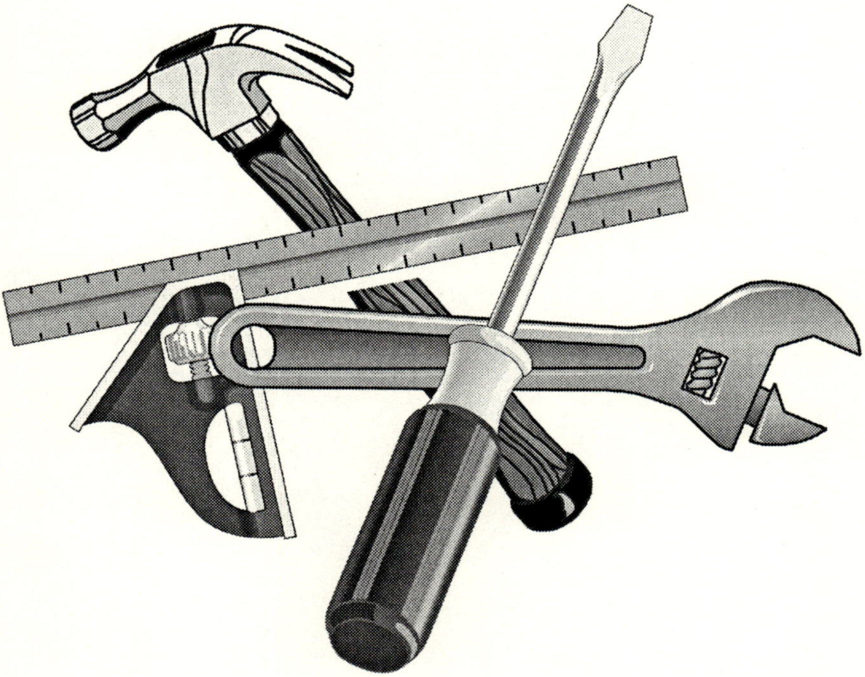

9
Additional Tools to Enhance Your Success

Winning is a habit. Unfortunately, so is losing.
Vince Lombardi (1913–1970)

As we come to the end of this book, I would like to equip you with some additional ideas that will help you maintain a strong focus on your goals and accelerate your achieving them.

It is a good habit to review the following ideas on a monthly basis:

- Review your master list of goals, and prioritize them from most important (one on a ten-point scale) to least important (on the same scale). Set dates for when you expect to reach these goals and note your progress on each one.

- You might need to adjust the expected date of achieving your goals.

- Keep your master list of goals concise, and keep the previous update so that you can see your progress and your deadline as well.

- Repeat the three-step exercise for the most important goals until you get them. You can apply the law of attraction for more than one goal at a time, but they should be from different aspects of life. For example, if you have a health goal, then you can run a wealth goal simultaneously. Avoid activating two goals from the same aspect, as this will provide you with more focus and concentration on your goal of that particular aspect.

- Keep a small note card [same size as credit card] and put your top three goals on this card. Develop a positive objective statement for each goal as described in the three-step exercise for the statement wording. Check this card at least three times daily by reading your three statements. Remember that the statement should use present tense and should be a very clear statement—as if you have already achieved your goals.

- Reward yourself if you achieved one of your goals or moved closer toward achievement.

- Inform your loved ones and friends once you have achieved a goal. Sharing your success with others will create a successful image that you want to keep in their mind about you. This will bring you more luck and will encourage them to seek your help.
- Help others achieve their goals. This will reflect back toward you and make others help you achieve your own goals in return.
- Repeat this statement each morning, "I am a successful person now."
- Repeat this statement each night, "I have achieved and learned a lot today. I cannot wait for a wonderful day tomorrow morning."
- Have a notebook to collect quotes about your success. You will have wonderful statements that will energize you as you move forward on the road of success and achievement.
- Search for a good hobby that you like and enjoy. This will provide you with relaxation on your journey to success. Also, you will maximize the use of your time even during your pleasure time.
- Set one bad habit on a piece of paper and work out a plan to replace it with a good one in two months. If you eliminate one bad habit every two months, you will eliminate six bad habits a year and sixty bad habits in ten years. You will be an entirely different person, with so many high qualities in ten years.
- Visit the library in your area and look for resources and materials related to your goals. This will broaden your vision and will open new ventures and methods to get your goals much easier and faster than you ever thought possible.
- Plan to attend seminars and courses on self-development. This will boost your ability to achieve your goals.

- From time to time, set a time to read stories of successful people and to learn from them.
- Listen to audio and watch video programs that talk about success and successful people.
- Your appearance is a very important reflection of your inside, so dress for success.
- Set one hour aside every week to see if you are really doing what you like in your life. This might reflect in enhancing your goals or even replacing them with more important goals for your true happiness.

Summary Points and Insight of Chapter 9:

- The best way to make a major achievement is to expand your experience and knowledge base.

- Training and learning work like a polish for you to shine more and more.

- Your appearance is a message to others about your inside.

- Get used to eliminating bad habits and replacing them with good ones.

- Have a hobby; your mind needs to play!!

One Final Word

I have tried my best to make this manual of success as concise as possible so that you can read it more than once. Also, its brevity will make it easier for you to keep it as a quick reference for goal achievement. I am sure that your commitment to the exercises and your utilization of the tools mentioned in this book will make a huge difference in your life and in getting what you want at amazing speed. You truly will see no goal beyond your reach. You will have full control of your life in a very smooth way.

I am absolutely confident that you will be much happier as you attain healthier mind and body, greater wealth, a deeper love of others, and better luck.

Once you complete reading this book, practicing the techniques outlined throughout, and have achieved your goals, then my wish is that you share your experiences with me and your friends. I welcome all your comments, as this will give me the opportunity to learn more from you.

I will be waiting to hear about your achievements and success stories very soon.

I hope to meet with you again in a higher dimension of a quality life.

References and Recommended Materials

The list below includes books, CDs, and DVDs.

1. Brian Tracy. *The Psychology of Achievement: Develop the Top Achiever's Mindset*, CD.

2. Brian Tracy. *Goals!: How to Get Everything You Want—Faster Than You Ever Thought Possible*, CD.

3. Brian Tracy. *Master Strategies for Higher Achievement: Set Your Goals and Reach Them—Fast!*, CD.

4. Brian Tracy. *Eat That Frog! 21 Great Ways to Stop Procrastinating and Get More Done in Less Time*, CD.

5. Brian Tracy. *Million Dollar Habits*.

6. Brian Tracy. *Create Your Own Future: How to Master the 12 Critical Factors of Unlimited Success*.

7. Norman Vincent Peale. *The Power of Positive Thinking*.

8. Sandra Anne Taylor. *Secrets of Attraction: The Universal Laws of Love, Sex and Romance*.

9. R. H. Jarrett. *It Works*.

10. Joseph Murphy. *The Power of Your Subconscious Mind*.

11. Bernie S. Siegel. *Love, Medicine, and Miracles: Lessons Learned about Self-Healing from a Surgeon's Experience with Exceptional Patients.*

12. Bernie S. Siegel. *Peace, Love and Healing: Bodymind Communication & the Path to Self-Healing: An Exploration.*

13. Michael Losier. *Law of Attraction.*

14. Esther Hicks and Jerry Hicks. *Ask & It Is Given: The Law (Ask and It Is Given).*

15. Peter F. Drucker. *The Daily Drucker: 366 Days of Insight and Motivation for Getting the Right Things Done.*

16. Anthony Robbins. *Awaken The Giant Within*, CD.

17. Lynn Grabhorn. *Excuse Me, Your Life is Waiting: The Astonishing Power of Feelings.*

18. Brian Tracy. *Brian Tracy's 21 Secrets to Success*, CD.

19. Kevin Hogan, Mary Lee Labay, and Jack Swaney. *Irresistible Attraction: Secrets of Personal Magnetism.*

20. Henriette Anne Klauser. *Write It Down, Make It Happen: Knowing What You Want And Getting It.*

21. Barbel Mohr. *The Cosmic Ordering Service.*

22. Anthony Robbins. *Introduction to Anthony Robbins Personal Power II*, CD.

23. Anthony Robbins. *Unlimited Power*, CD.

24. Robert Dilts. *Modeling With NLP.*

25. Stephen R. Covey. *Focus: Achieving Your Highest Priorities*, CD.

26. Anthony Robbins. *Lessons in Mastery*, CD.

27. Tony Buzan. *Use Both Sides of Your Brain.*

28. Colin G Smith. *The Original NLP Toolbox.*

29. Ibrahim Elfiky. *NLP & Unlimited Communication Power.*

References on the Web

1. http://www.success.org
2. http://www.success.com
3. http://www.iloveulove.com/psychology/univlaws.htm
4. http://www.nlp-now.co.uk/learn-nlp.htm
5. http://www.nlpschedule.com/random/research-summary.html
6. http://library.thinkquest.org/17360/tb-e-con.html
7. http://alcoholism.about.com/od/brain/
8. http://www.successconsciousness.com/index_000009.htm
9. http://www.wealthbeyondreason.com/
10. http://www.thinkexist.com/English/Author/x/Author_1082_3.htm
11. http://www.over1000000.com

Arabic References (Titles were translated from Arabic to English)

1. Salah Alrashed. *Effective Change*, audiotape.
2. Salah Alrashed. *Positive Thinking*.
3. Salah Alrashed. *Get What You Want*.
4. Salah Alrashed. *Happiness in Three Months*.
5. Ibrahim Elfiky. *Unlimited Success*, audiotape.

6. Ibrahim Elfiky. *Laws of Subconscious Mind*, video.

7. Ibrahim Elfiky. *The Power of Self-Confidence*, video.

8. Ibrahim Elfiky. *The Power of Self-Control*, video.

9. Ibrahim Elfiky. *The Art and Secrets of Decision Making*, video.

APPENDIX A

Exercise 1

Day 1   **January 1, 2006**

1. I have one hundred thousand dollars in my account now.
2. I have one hundred thousand dollars in my account now.
3. I have one hundred thousand dollars in my account now.
4. I have one hundred thousand dollars in my account now.
5. I have one hundred thousand dollars in my account now.
6. I have one hundred thousand dollars in my account now.
7. I have one hundred thousand dollars in my account now.
8. I have one hundred thousand dollars in my account now.
9. I have one hundred thousand dollars in my account now.
10. I have one hundred thousand dollars in my account now.
11. I have one hundred thousand dollars in my account now.
12. I have one hundred thousand dollars in my account now.
13. I have one hundred thousand dollars in my account now.
14. I have one hundred thousand dollars in my account now.
15. I have one hundred thousand dollars in my account now.
16. I have one hundred thousand dollars in my account now.

17. I have one hundred thousand dollars in my account now.
18. I have one hundred thousand dollars in my account now.
19. I have one hundred thousand dollars in my account now.
20. I have one hundred thousand dollars in my account now.
21. I have one hundred thousand dollars in my account now.

Exercise 1

Day 2   **January 2, 2006**

1. I have one hundred thousand dollars in my account now.
2. I have one hundred thousand dollars in my account now.
3. I have one hundred thousand dollars in my account now.
4. I have one hundred thousand dollars in my account now.
5. I have one hundred thousand dollars in my account now.
6. I have one hundred thousand dollars in my account now.
7. I have one hundred thousand dollars in my account now.
8. I have one hundred thousand dollars in my account now.
9. I have one hundred thousand dollars in my account now.
10. I have one hundred thousand dollars in my account now.
11. I have one hundred thousand dollars in my account now.
12. I have one hundred thousand dollars in my account now.
13. I have one hundred thousand dollars in my account now.
14. I have one hundred thousand dollars in my account now.
15. I have one hundred thousand dollars in my account now.
16. I have one hundred thousand dollars in my account now.
17. I have one hundred thousand dollars in my account now.
18. I have one hundred thousand dollars in my account now.
19. I have one hundred thousand dollars in my account now.
20. I have one hundred thousand dollars in my account now.

21. I have one hundred thousand dollars in my account now.

You will need to make a new sheet for each day. The last sheet follows on the next page.

Exercise 1

Day 21 [Last Day]   **January 21, 2006**

1. I have one hundred thousand dollars in my account now.
2. I have one hundred thousand dollars in my account now.
3. I have one hundred thousand dollars in my account now.
4. I have one hundred thousand dollars in my account now.
5. I have one hundred thousand dollars in my account now.
6. I have one hundred thousand dollars in my account now.
7. I have one hundred thousand dollars in my account now.
8. I have one hundred thousand dollars in my account now.
9. I have one hundred thousand dollars in my account now.
10. I have one hundred thousand dollars in my account now.
11. I have one hundred thousand dollars in my account now.
12. I have one hundred thousand dollars in my account now.
13. I have one hundred thousand dollars in my account now.
14. I have one hundred thousand dollars in my account now.
15. I have one hundred thousand dollars in my account now.
16. I have one hundred thousand dollars in my account now.
17. I have one hundred thousand dollars in my account now.
18. I have one hundred thousand dollars in my account now.
19. I have one hundred thousand dollars in my account now.
20. I have one hundred thousand dollars in my account now.

21. I have one hundred thousand dollars in my account now.

This will be the last day of exercise one, which is on day 21.

Exercise 1—Blank Sample

Day **Date:**

1.
2.
3.
4.
5.
6.
7.
8.
9.
10.
11.
12.
13.
14.
15.
16.
17.
18.
19.
20.
21.

APPENDIX B

Exercise 2

Day 8 (First Day of Exercise 2)   **January 8, 2006**

Visualize that you have a certain amount of money. Think what you might do to invest it and whether you can double it in six months. Imagine how much you could have one year from now, as you have already achieved the first one hundred thousand dollars.

Exercise 2

Day 9　　　　　　　　　　　　　　　**January 9, 2006**

Continue your visualization that you achieved for the one hundred thousand dollars and continue thinking about possible investment opportunities. Imagine how much you might make in the next two years. Grow your dreams as you progress, and this will open new options.

You will need to make a new sheet for each day. The last sheet follows on the next page.

Exercise 2

Day 21 **January 21, 2006**

[Day 14 of Exercise 2 which is the last day of this exercise]

Imagine the things you can do with the amount you have already achieved. Imagine building your dream house, purchasing your desired car, and having established a better job—or even your own business.

This will be the last day of exercise two, which takes place on day 21 of the program.

APPENDIX C

Exercise 3

Day 15 (First Day of Exercise 3)   **January 15, 2006**

Remember the first day of the exercise and how many things happen to you to bring you closer to your objective. List your achievement here, and do not ignore even a program on the TV or radio or a magazine that talked about your goal. Even write down your talks with your friends about new business ventures and so on. Basically, appreciate any small or big sign that indicates your achievement toward your goal.

Exercise 3

Day 21   **January 21, 2006**

(Day 7 of Exercise 3 which is the last day of this exercise)

This will be the last day of exercise three, which is day 21 of the program.

APPENDIX D

Ten-Year Goals

This table is for the ten-year category. You must review it yearly at a minimum. This table is called the "Vision."

Importance	Description	Step-by-step strategy	Percent complete	Review date	Completion date
1.					
2.					
3.					
4.					
5.					
6.					
7.					
8.					
9.					
10.					

Five-Year Goals

This table is for five-year goals. You must review it once every six months at a minimum. This table is called "The Road Map."

Importance	Description	Step-by-step strategy	Percent complete	Review date	Completion date
1.					
2.					
3.					
4.					
5.					
6.					
7.					
8.					
9.					
10.					

One-Year Goals

This table is for the one-year category. You must review it monthly at a minimum. This table is called "My Plans for This Year."

Importance	Description	Step-by-step strategy	Percent complete	Review date	Completion date
1.					
2.					
3.					
4.					
5.					
6.					
7.					
8.					
9.					
10.					

Appendix E

Sample Statements for the Law of Attraction

Samples of statements to activate law of attraction:

- I am enjoying a great love with my partner right now.
- I have established my own one-million-dollar business now.
- I am loved by others right now.
- I am the head of the department right now.
- I have achieved my bachelor degree in mathematics with highest honors.
- I am an excellent speaker who attracts his audience immediately right now.
- I have a wonderful relationship with coworkers right now.
- I own my dream house right now.
- I speak Spanish fluently and easily right now.
- I am a very lucky person in life.
- I have won the best worker prize of the year.
- I love my children as they mean everything in my life.
- I am maintaining a healthy body right now.
- I am a social star wherever I go right now.

- I am gifted with wisdom when I think, talk, and act.
- I am a very well-known doctor in my practice of medicine in my city right now.
- I have a trim, slim, and fit body right now.

Index

alcohol consumption, 27
attraction, law of. *See* law of attraction
auditory personality, 49, 50

Bandler, Richard, 46
belief system
    metaphor and, 48–49
    trigger for change, 47–48
breathing techniques, 27–28

cause and effect, law of, 18–19
coaches, 56
communication
    and personality types, 49–50
    representation of (*see* neuro-
        linguistic programming)
concentration, law of, 20
correspondence, law of, 19

equivalent thinking, law of, 20
expectation, law of, 20

global energy theory, 19
goal achievement
    and law of attraction, 36–41
    models, use of, 50–51
    tools for, 62–64
goal setting, 2–4
    for financial independence, 25–26
    regular review of, 62
Grinder, John, 46

health, and law of attraction, 26–28

kinesthetic personality, 49, 50

law of attraction
    and goal achievement, 36–41
    real-life examples, 30–32
    sample statements to activate, 93–94
    success, aspects of, 24–30
law of cause and effect, 18–19
law of concentration, 20
law of correspondence, 19
law of equivalent thinking, 20
law of expectation, 20
law of the subconscious mind, 19–20
learning style, and personality, 49–50
love, and law of attraction, 28–29
luck, and law of attraction, 29–30

mentors, 56
metaphor, and belief system, 48–49

negative energy, 14
neuro-linguistic programming, 19–20
    and belief system, 47–49
    overview, 46–47
    and personality types, 49–50

personality types, 49–50
positive energy, 14
positive thinking process, 18

quantum physics, 8

smoking, effects of, 27
subconscious mind, law of the, 19–20
success, sharing of, 56–57

thinking process, 14

positive, 18

time management, for health, 26–27

universal laws. *See* individual entries

visual personality, 49, 50

wealth, and law of attraction, 25–26

978-0-595-38363-4
0-595-38363-7

Printed in the United Kingdom
by Lightning Source UK Ltd.
119646UK00001B/395